A Precious Life

A Precious Life

A Jataka Tale

Illustrated by Rosalyn White

DHARMA PUBLISHING

Jataka Tales Series

Second edition 2009, revised and augmented with guidance for parents and teachers.

Printed on acid-free paper.

Printed in the United States of America by Dharma Press 35788 Hauser Bridge Road, Cazadero, California 95421.

9   8   7   6   5   4   3   2   1

Library of Congress Control Number: 2009936419
ISBN 978-0-89800-512-7

www.dharmapublishing.com

Dedicated to children everywhere

Long ago in the land of India there was a deserted forest through which no travelers ever passed because the grass was high, and thick shrubs grew between the trees. Many small animals made a safe home among the bushes, and hundreds of birds built their nests in the leafy trees. In these woods also lived a great being in the form of a deer.

One day when the ruler of the land was out on a hunt, he spied the rich greenery and the shadowy depths of the deep forest. "What a perfect hunting ground!" he declared. "So many animals must live among those trees!" And into the forest he dashed, his riding companions trailing him in their jeweled chariots. But soon the chariots were caught in the tangled brush, leaving the king to continue his ride all alone.

Spurring his horse through the brush, the king plunged deeper and deeper into the woods. Terrified animals fled to all sides. Suddenly, in the distance, he spotted the great deer. "Hmmm!" he thought. "What a magnificent creature! I have never seen a deer of such fine color and form. What a prize he would be!" The king reached for his bow, strung it with a deadly arrow, and urged his horse into a gallop.

When the deer saw rider and horse approaching, he took flight in great leaps and bounds. The king could not take his eyes off the deer, so graceful and strong were his movements as he fled among the bushes and trees. Coming upon a gaping ravine, the deer simply bounded across it and ran on without missing a beat. But the king's horse reared up and stopped dead in its tracks. The king flew out of his saddle and tumbled headlong over the edge of the cliff.

No longer hearing the horse's hooves behind, him the deer thought, "Perhaps the hunter has ended his chase." But when he looked back, there was the riderless horse standing at the edge of the ravine. The deer quickly realized the fate of his pursuer. While an ordinary animal would have run for its life, relieved to escape, the deer felt only pity.

"Perhaps the fall has broken his bones. Perhaps he is lying there, moaning in pain! Alone and injured, far from the help of his friends, he must be in great torment. Accustomed to comfort and good fortune, he is now desperate and frightened. How can I desert him? If he is still alive, he will never be able to escape all by himself."

The deer walked back to the ravine and looked over the edge. At the bottom lay the king, his eyes closed in pain, his tunic torn and covered with dirt, his jeweled crown and his fine bow and arrows scattered around him as if they were discarded toys. Seeing the king suffering and in pain, the deer spoke to him gently: "I hope you have not come to great harm. Please, do not hesitate to trust in me. I have the power to rescue you. If you would like me to help you, simply say so and I shall come to your aid."

To hear such kind words from an animal touched the king deeply. Suddenly he was filled with shame. "How can you show mercy to me who was intent on killing you? And how could I have thought to kill such an innocent and gentle creature? It is I who am the beast and you who are the king! But how will you rescue me? I fear I am doomed to die in this miserable pit, just as I deserve."

But the deer was undaunted. He looked around for ways to help the king. First he found a rock the weight of a man and slid it onto his back. Then he practiced carrying the heavy rock up and down gullies and along narrow ledges, until he could balance it perfectly. When he was confident that he could bear the weight of the man without slipping, he descended into the ravine.

"Mount my back as if I were your horse and hold on to my neck," explained the deer. When the king was securely astride, the deer jumped up the cliff in a flash.

"My life is yours!" exclaimed the king. "Ask of me anything within my power and I will grant it. Please, come live in my palace and be my friend. Leave this dreadful forest where another might soon come to hunt you."

"My only wish," replied the deer, "is that you stop your hunting forever, O King. The poor animals that live in the forest deserve your pity, not your arrows. Though they may not have the same intelligence as men, animals have the same feelings. They too want happiness and fear suffering. Is it not wrong to do to others what you do not wish others to do to you?"

From that day forward the king renounced hunting. Treating all creatures as he would wish to be treated, he became famous for his care of the smallest birds and insects, the fiercest of animals, and both the good and wicked among men. Realizing that each life is precious and that any being he met might be a great being, he treated all creatures with kindness and respect.

The Jataka Tales nurture in readers young and old an appreciation for values shared by all the world's great traditions. Read aloud, performed and studied for centuries, they communicate universal values such as kindness, forgiveness, compassion, humility, courage, honesty and patience. You can bring these stories alive through the suggestions on these pages. Actively engaging with the stories creates a bridge to the children in your life and opens a dialogue about what brings joy, stability and caring.

A Precious Life

A king, out hunting a deer, falls from his horse and is trapped in a deep ravine. Seeing the hunter's plight, the deer risks his own life to carry the hunter to safety. To repay the deer for his kindness, the king respects the deer's wish that all forest creatures be safe from his arrows. He vows to become the protector of all the animals.

Key Values
Empathy, Respect, Kindness, Helping Others, Nonviolence, Resourcefulness

Bringing the story to life

Engage the children by saying, "This story takes place in a deep forest where a wise deer lives. One day a king who loves hunting rides into the forest. What do you think happens when he sees the deer? Let's read to find out."

• How did the king end up in the ravine?
• How did the deer react to being chased? What happened afterward?
• What changes the king's thinking about hunting?
• How does the deer train to help the king?
• What would you like to learn that could help you or someone else?
• What does the king vow to do at the end of the story?

Discussion topics and questions can be modified depending on the child's age

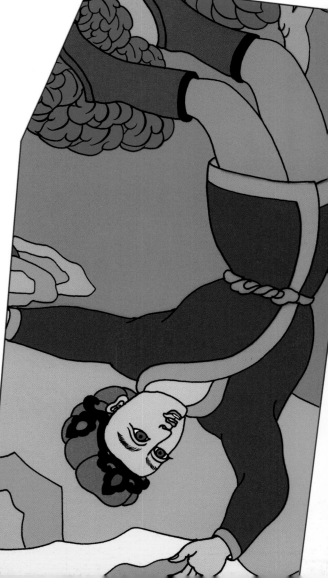

Teaching values through play

Follow up on the storytelling with creative activities that explore the characters and values and appeal to the five senses.

- Have the children construct and decorate character masks for the deer and the king. Act out the story, and then have the children switch roles (from hunter-king to the one who saves the hunter) and ask: "Would you save someone who had wanted to hunt you?" And "Why does the deer save the king?"

- Children can play at being skilled, useful adults who help others. Remind them that the deer trains to save the king by carrying rocks on his back. Let them play a fireperson, a doctor, a teacher, a president, for example.

- Have the children retell the story in their own words from the point of view of the king. They can explore how the king promises not to hunt anymore.

- The children can make up different endings, including one where the deer doesn't save the hunter-king. What then?

Active reading

- Before children can read, they enjoy story telling and love growing familiar with the characters and drawings. You can just show them the pictures and tell the story in your own words with characteristic voices for each animal.

- By reading the book to them two or three times and helping them to recognize words, you help them build vocabulary.

- Carry a book whenever you leave the house in case there is some extra time for reading.

- Display the key values on the refrigerator or a bulletin board – at child's eye level – and refer to them in your daily interactions.

- Ask the children about a time when someone treated them with kindness, even when they were angry or upset. See if the children can remember when they began to appreciate that caring treatment.

Daily activities

When cooking or taking out the garbage, have children think about themes such as recycling. Ask them, "Would the king have recycled his garbage before he met the deer?"

When you are out, start noticing animals that help human beings. Ask the children, "Can you think of animals upon whom people rely?" Get more information from this National Geographic article: http://news.national-geographic.com/news/2002/08/0808_020808_therapydogs.html or visit http://www.tdi-dog.org/ for stories about animals helping in the world today.

We are grateful for the opportunity to offer these Jataka tales to you. May they inspire fresh insight into the dynamics of human relationships and may understanding grow with each reading.

These adaptations of Jataka Tales are for children aged three to eight

JATAKA TALES SERIES